YO-AUL-594

Southwestern Studies

Monograph No. 9

Pancho Villa at Columbus
The Raid of 1916

by

HALDEEN BRADDY

Southwestern Studies

VOLUME III   Spring, 1965   NUMBER 1

SAMUEL D. MYRES, *Editor*

Issued at El Paso by the
TEXAS WESTERN COLLEGE PRESS

Pancho Villa at Columbus
The Raid of 1916

by

HALDEEN BRADDY

MONOGRAPH NO. 9

COPYRIGHT 1965
TEXAS WESTERN COLLEGE

EDITORIAL BOARD

S. D. Myres, *Chairman*

C. L. Sonnichsen   Ray Small   W. H. Timmons

J. M. Sharp   J. H. Haddox   R. Milton Leech

Carl Hertzog, *Director of the Press*

ABOUT THE AUTHOR

Haldeen Braddy is Professor of English, Texas Western College. A native of East Texas, he holds the A.B. degree from East Texas State Teachers College, the M.A. from The University of Texas, and the Ph.D. from New York University.

A recognized authority on American folklore, Dr. Braddy has devoted much attention to the Southwestern scene. His research on Pancho Villa began thirty years ago while Braddy was head of the English department at Sul Ross College, Alpine, Texas. He initiated at that time a study of the *guerrillero* by preparing an article that appeared in the *Southwest Review* in 1937. Later, he produced ten other essays, an article for the *Encyclopedia Americana*, and a book, *Cock of the Walk*, on the revolutionary leader.

The monograph printed here is a result of Dr. Braddy's continuing interest in the subject. This account of the Columbus raid is a reevaluation of that incident, made possible after a half century by the discovery of new materials and the achievement of a better perspective.

The following study first reviews Villa's background, his earlier anti-American acts, and the deep-seated hostility toward *gringos* that motivated him. It next describes the Mexican leader's moves in organizing and carrying out the raid; it then reviews the American defense and the forced retreat of the Villistas. Finally, it appraises the incident from the standpoint of its purpose and its historical significance.

The views expressed in *Southwestern Studies* are those of the authors and not necessarily of the College Press.

PANCHO VILLA AT COLUMBUS
The Raid of 1916 Restudied

By HALDEEN BRADDY

CONFLICTING early rumors about Francisco (Pancho) Villa's descent on Columbus, New Mexico, March 9, 1916, have led writers since then to interpret the Raid as mainly an act of terrorism. Debate has also arisen over such pertinent matters as the number of Villistas who crossed the border, the role of Villa himself in the sortie, the failure or success of his plans, and the possible political motives behind the incursion. Viewed today in the retrospect of the past fifty years, the rumors and controversies of that time can now be evaluated more objectively, and major truths can at last be established firmly.

One reason for this claim is that the personal account of General John J. Pershing, lately made available for public examination, throws clear light on what happened at Columbus. Equally valuable new data in the form of oral and written testimony from both American and Mexican survivors also bear pertinently on the activities of Villa that led to the climax in New Mexico.[1] The paradoxes of the Raid may finally be resolved within the context of Villa's career as a Mexican guerrilla. Only with this approach can one construe rationally the events of that fateful morning of March 9. The Villista assault on New Mexico soil will be expounded here as the natural result of the minor incidents which preceded it.

Villa Becomes a Guerrilla

Pancho Villa became a fugitive from the Carrancista regime after crucial encounters with two of Venustiano Carranza's generals in the field, Alvaro Obregón and Plutarco Elías Calles. Obregón defeated Villa overwhelmingly in the southern Guanajuato capital,

Celaya, in April, 1915. Calles routed him in the northwestern state of Sonora at Agua Prieta in November. Reeling back from these debacles in the south and in the north, Villa retreated eastward to central Chihuahua in December, when he disbanded his demoralized army. Approximately five hundred devoted followers remained with him to form a guerrilla band. Thereafter, though still enjoying considerable popular support, Villa the marauder was obliged to forage for both funds and supplies.

The United States, which formally recognized Carranza as *Presidente* in October, 1915, was interested in seeing peace restored in Mexico. Disturbed conditions there during the Revolution posed a threat to American investments. A pressing problem in the northern Mexican states arose from roving bands of looters who plundered native-owned properties and, sometimes, foreign holdings. Moreover, in 1915 Mexican marauders even wrecked a passenger train in Texas, killing several Americans near Brownsville. This attack, outside Villa's normal range, was typical; and others like it followed. Raids like these, often occurring at widely separated points, had to be the work of several bandit chiefs, not of any single one.

The most feared of such *jefes* was Pancho Villa. Mobile as his men were — and they roved wider than their fellows — it would have been physically impossible for them to commit all the depredations attributed to them. Villa's name nonetheless became synonymous with "marauder." In the opinion of General Pershing, Villistas bore the guilt for the main boundary violations. Pershing noted also that Villa pillaged American ranches and settlements at Red House Ferry, Progress Post Office, and Las Paladas — all within a few months; he observed that the invader then escaped punishment in both Mexico and the United States. Again, the American general charged that ruthless bestiality and savage acts of mutilation characterized the assaults.[2] The Villa rovers respected neither God nor woman and bitterly hated the aliens in their country. In some instances, "The blonde women of the passive Mennonites fell prey to their violence. According to one indictment, Mennonites were particularly attractive to the Villistas, who made a sport of raping the young women in front of their men, who, true to their religion, could only watch and pray."[3]

It would serve no purpose to expand on Villa's various exploits, particularly those unauthenticated. The great concern of the United States of course centered on American-owned ranches and mines located in Mexico. Relations between the two countries suffered crises at different times during the Revolution. Shortly after its outbreak, a crisis involving El Paso developed from battle operations in Juárez. This occurred in 1911 when bullets from the warring revolutionaries killed and wounded Americans north of the Rio Grande. When the Americans asked for Federal protection, Washington allegedly wired in reply: "If El Pasoans are being killed, let them move out of the line of fire."[4]

The government at Washington had difficulty in evaluating the situation or narrowing down the culpability to any one Mexican leader. Certainly, not all the border terrorists were Villistas. For one instance, on September 23, 1915, troops commanded by a Carranza officer crossed the lower Rio Grande to attack a patrol of American soldiers, and in the short skirmish killed two of them. For another, in the following month a Carrancista soldier, in the same area, wantonly murdered an American and displayed his severed head on a pole for all to see.[5]

As a bonafide leader of one of the dominant political parties, Villa could not be summarily branded by the United States as a simple brigand and officially prosecuted. The problem of the American government in dealing with Villa was his nigh-universal popularity with the Mexican masses, who regarded him as a sincere patriot. Many of the men who rode with Villa shared with him the distinction of having fought in the Revolution from the beginning. Few, if any, of these men belonged to the criminal class. Largely unknown to American readers, the names of these men and their backgrounds have a relevant place in the chronicling of the Columbus Raid.

At the outset, Villa's men, sombreroed *hombres* with khaki-colored uniforms and criss-cross bandoliers over their deep chests, included such officers as squat Tomás Urbina, tall Candelario

Cervantes, and slender Pablo López. The Villistas soon included peons of low estate as well as aristocrats like Don Felipe Angeles. These bold men stood ready to die for Villa, and die for him many of them did. Some of them survived the raid in New Mexico to live with him later in Durango at Rancho Canutillo. This group of survivors comprised Lorenzo Avalos, Ramón Contreras, Ramón Córdoba, Daniel Delgado, Nicolás Fernández, José García, Sóstenes Garza, Alfonso Gómez, José M. Jaurrieta, José Nieto, Ricardo Michel, Pánfilo Ornelas, Ernesto Ríos, Silverio Tabares, Daniel Tamayo, and Miguel Trillo.[6] Others of the raiders fought with Villa through the years, such as, it is believed, Martín López and Juan Salas. They had been mainstays of a gang of outlaws headed by a robber named Parra.

Pancho Villa began his career, it is claimed, when he inherited the Parra band. When the Revolution broke out, Villa recruited another group as patriots instead of as bandits. The most famous of these belonged to a select group called the *Dorados* (the Golden Ones). Candelario Cervantes, who figured prominently at Columbus, was his most trusted *Dorado* officer. With his lieutenants, Villa shared all that he had, and he sometimes entrusted to them many decisions. Once the Golden Ones had sported khaki uniforms and colorful bands on their steeple-crowned sombreros, but the majority of raiders who rode with Villa to Columbus were a ragtag assortment of Mexican peons, *muchachos* fourteen to sixteen years old,[7] and fierce Yaqui Indians — a desert rabble from Chihuahua and Sonora.

Early Anti-American Acts

Ripe pickings for these guerrillas were the American-owned mining properties. The leader Villa, unmolested by the Mexican authorities,[8] was a tried hand at this kind of harvest. Even before the Revolution, he had learned how to extract *dinero* from unfortunate miners in sheer banditry. In June, 1909, in San José del Sitio, Chihuahua, seven bandits arrived at the *hacienda mayor* of William W. Tuttle and Mike Farrel. These two Americans had charge of the Pittsburgh-San José Reduction and Railroad Company, located at the edge of the town. At about 6:30 P.M. the seven brigands rode up and, without a word, began to batter the two miners with rifle butts. Mr. Tuttle attempted to resist with his fists, but neither victim had a chance against their seven armed assailants. After being beaten into unconsciousness, Tuttle and Farrel were bound hand and foot and were searched for valuables. The robbers confiscated everything, even the clothes the two men wore, as well as all garments and linen found in the house. Official investigators named the assailants as Villa, Tomás Urbina, Anselmo Solares, Feliciano Domínguez, two brothers named López, and José Jesús Sánchez.[9]

By 1915 Villa's sadistic attacks had so intimidated the miners that he could extort money simply by threats. Edward Plumb, chief employee of the El Potosí Company (in Chihuahua City) kept $50,000 in gold in his room to pay the bandit for protection. If not paid, Villa saw to it that the mines ceased operation. Sometimes he did this by stealing the fuel; sometimes he abducted the mine operator. In one celebrated later case, he kidnapped Frank Knotts, who operated the Erupción Mining Company near Villa Ahumada, Chihuahua, and released him only after the payment of an exorbitant ransom.[10]

The most infamous act perpetrated in Mexico against Americans has become known in the history of the Southwest as the Santa Isabel Massacre. On January 10, 1916, a group of Americans set out by train from Chihuahua City for the Cusi Mining Company, some distance away. The governor of Chihuahua had given this group of travelers official assurance of safe passage, providing them with passports and safe-conducts.

Near Santa Isabel, however, a band of Villistas stopped the train. The guerrillas forced fifteen Americans off the train and afterwards shot them to death, stripping the bodies naked and mutilating them.[11] Joe Miller, a fellow passenger, saw what happened inside the train but not outside, since he remained on it. He had this to say about the massacre:

Among the men on the train were Mr. Watson (6 feet 2 inches), manager of Cusi Mining, and a Mr. Anderson, at that time a young fellow. Then the train went on to Madera after it had been looted. The men were murdered after the train left. Colonel Domínguez, a Villista, led this attack. He was cross-eyed, about 5 feet 11 inches, and he was born in that part of the country.[12]

The motives behind this atrocity are not fully apparent. The United States claimed that Villa had planned the bloodletting. Perhaps the Mexican leader felt frustrated because the United States had not recognized him instead of Carranza. There is a story that Villa had warned the victims to stay away from the Cusi properties. Despite their disregard of the warning, he denied responsibility for their deaths. American officials nevertheless unequivocally cited Pancho and his *compañeros* as the culprits:

TELEGRAM

Special Agent Silliman to the Secretary of State

Querétaro, January 19, 1916

"The text has been furnished me of a decree declaring that on account of connections with the Santa Isabel massacre Francisco Villa, Rafael Castro and Pablo López are outside the law, and that any citizen may apprehend and execute them, the only formality being their identification."[13]

Four days after the Santa Isabel massacre, when in El Paso civilians began to riot and to attack the Mexican quarter of the city, General Pershing had to deploy his troops to maintain order. Upon the arrival in El Paso of the mutilated corpses from Santa Isabel, the American citizenry became so inflamed that the General declared martial law. The barbarous outrage not only infuriated El Pasoans, but also provoked indignant cries for redress all along the Texas border. Had the Americans taken direct action against Villa promptly, the Columbus raid probably never would have occurred.

An informant reported that the Villistas at Santa Isabel also sabercut a dog belonging to the Americans. The animal survived his lacerations and ran yelping away to spread the tale of gore and terror. In addition, a gold ring taken off the corpse of a Mr. Newman at Santa Isabel was later retrieved from the hand of a Mexican raider killed at Columbus.[14]

After the massacre of the American travelers, Villa consistently disavowed that either he or his men had had anything to do with such a heinous crime.[15] As incriminating facts began to add up, placing his men at the scene of the killing, he asserted that José Rodríguez and Pablo López, his lieutenants, had acted strictly on their own in the Santa Isabel incident. Partly to assuage American indignation, the Carranza government early in 1916 executed Villa's minion, José Rodríguez, as the guilty party. When López later met his execution in April for having led the massacre, he named his chief, Villa, as the person responsible.

The failure of either the Carrancista or the American government to contain Villa and to restrict his ravaging soon bore its strange fruit at Columbus. Since he had eluded punishment, he flouted both governments, interpreting their passivity as deference to his political strength. Even so, Villa played it safe, staying pretty much out of the public view for an intermission of weeks. By now, the confiscated American mines remained unworked and no longer yielded plunder. Also, he lacked the manpower to battle the Carrancistas for the purpose of capturing food and supplies. Still proscribed by Carranza and Obregón, whose prestige grew by the day, the Mexican irregular found his territory more and more constricted. To revive his defeated band into a military force, he needed more bounty than the ravaged Mexican countryside had to offer. In those long days before the Columbus raid, the gnawings of hunger made the hard-pressed guerrillas restless and sparked their longing for action and the smell of gunpowder.

How could the guerrilla *jefe* appease the growing discontent of his hungry pack and yet not jeopardize his own personal safety? Still a fugitive, he had to avoid being identified specifically as a participator in acts of provocation. Meanwhile, he and his company of outcasts needed to keep on the move to escape the vigilant eye of the Carranza forces. Carranza daily waxed stronger in his determination to impress the United States that he was in control of the entire country and able to restore peace by holding all rebellious elements in check.

Villa, as the only chief with substantial popular appeal, clearly had a problem on his hands. In the Revolution his presence at the head of his charging cavalry had created the idealized image of a fearless and intrepid officer. He had required that his lieutenants display equal bravery and daring. In those days wherever there was fighting, there was sure to be Villa. The epitome of action, he allowed no time for *siestas* in his army and introduced night fighting as a new concept in Mexican warfare. His swift and audacious attacks earned for him the nickname "The Lion of the North."

As a harried irregular, *"El León del Norte"* had to follow the pack and direct it from out of sight. He had learned this new technique after he had led his old-style cavalry charges to disaster against the entrenched Obregón forces early in 1915. Perhaps this explains why he did not appear in person at Santa Isabel. This new knack was to figure in his decisions regarding the invasion at Columbus. His accomplices José Rodríguez and Pablo López, after trial and conviction, had paid for Santa Isabel with their lives — Villa himself had come away unscathed.

Villa's Motivation

Exactly why the guerrilla chieftain settled on a violation of the international line has always been a subject of controversy. A popular explanation among certain of Pershing's officers holds that "Villa raided Columbus for loot."[16] Was it for supplies and the spoils of war that he made the attack? The 13th Cavalry, with headquarters at Columbus, had exactly the supplies he required for his band. Plenty of machine guns, which he needed desperately, stood in stacks at the army camp there. Food and clothes, all kinds of provender, filled the military camp and the town's general stores.

Villa had carried on an extensive business with Sam and Louis Ravel's store in Columbus, purchasing large quantities of guns and ammunition. At the time, rumors circulated among Southwesterners that he had paid the Ravel brothers for a shipment of guns and ammunition which he had never received. As a matter of fact, one of the raiders later stated that Villa "was angry because he did not receive ammunition that he paid for there."[17] Recently an item in the El Paso *Herald-Post* supported this view, declaring

Pancho Villa at Columbus [11

that "Cervantes reported to Villa that Sam Ravel refused to sell him guns. He said that Ravel refused to return money left for a deal in 1913."[18]

Or perhaps the plain facts of history explain Villa's motivation. The policy of the United States in favoring Carranza meant the denial of munitions to Villa. The United States had allowed Carrancista units to travel by American railway through Texas and New Mexico from Piedras Negras, Coahuila, to Douglas, Arizona. There the Carrancistas crossed over to nearby Agua Prieta and in November, 1915, helped Calles to overcome the guerrilla forces. To minimize his defeat, Villa complained that he had lost the advantage of night attack when high-powered American searchlights in Douglas had focused on his troops, rendering them sitting-duck targets. It also has been advanced that "Another one of Villa's intentions at Columbus was to stop the train which ran from Douglas, Arizona, to El Paso, Texas, because the travelers on the train included the lawyers, Luis Cabrera and Roberto Pesqueira, who were returning from Sonora where they had assisted in the marriage of his enemy Alvaro Obregón."[19] Certainly, he hated his rival Obregón bitterly. But he never molested the train in Columbus, for it arrived after his retreat. The incident now seems unimportant; yet who could read the mind of Villa?

Possibly the American provocations inspired Villa's *Manifesto to the Nation*, issued at San Andrés, Chihuahua, in October, 1916. In it the frantic Conventionist leader proclaimed the Americans to be "Our eternal enemies ... and ... the barbarians of the North."[20] One aim of the Columbus fracas may have been to highlight Carranza's inability to police rebellious native elements and thus to undermine Woodrow Wilson's confidence in the newly recognized Mexican president. Indeed, two eminent Mexican historians state that Columbus was attacked as vengeance against Americans for recognizing Villa's enemy countryman Carranza.[21]

The truth is that Villa had precious few friends either foreign or domestic. A five-power conference of Argentina, Brazil, Chile, Guatemala, and Uruguay in August, 1915, had preferred Carranza to Villa. Moreover, twenty-nine of the thirty Mexican states now supported Carranza, Chihuahua alone backing Villa. In a solitary dissent, an American commander, General Hugh L. Scott, observes in his memoirs that the United States decided in favor of the wrong man: "The recognition of Carranza — by Wilson — had the effect of solidifying the power of the man who had rewarded us with kicks on every occasion, and of making an outlaw of the man who had helped us."[22]

Why, then, did Pancho Villa raid Columbus? He had a long list of grievances;[23] and in his then straitened situation any one of these would have sufficed to provoke him to this most desperate vengeance.

The citizens of El Paso, familiar with Villa's earlier rampages across the Rio Grande in neighboring Juárez, feared lest their city become the scene of his *venganza desesperada*. In fact, border residents constantly heard rumors to this effect. Their apprehension did not lack some basis, because the sister city had been Villa's favorite headquarters. For this reason, military authorities at nearby Fort Bliss remained on alert for a sudden attack.

[The residents of Columbus, in contrast, found less cause for alarm. Confident with their garrison of soldiers, they went about their daily tasks unworried that only a few miles south of them Villa might be preparing for attack. They reasoned that if an attack came, it would involve not Columbus, New Mexico, but her sister city south of the line, Palomas, Chihuahua. For a while after Santa Isabel, they vigilantly patrolled the borderline in their corner of New Mexico. After that, little by little, they relaxed their watch. In the month of March, 1916, Americans were never more vulnerable than at Columbus, but not so wholly vulnerable as Villa's spies reported. The scouts told their chief that the Americans had only a handful of troopers on guard.]

The net effect of Villa's apparent feinting toward El Paso, while in fact moving closer to Columbus, must have built up some element of surprise. On the very night of the attack Colonel Herbert J. Slocum, the Army chief at Columbus, had even gone out of town to Deming.

Organizing the Columbus Venture

In January, 1916, the size of Villa's band, according to intelligence reports, seemed unimpressive to the well armed American garrisons along the border. Villa, however, continued to add new men from the hour he left his headquarters at Hacienda San Gerónimo, Chihuahua, on February 27. Actually, by one means or another, scores of chance recruits filled out the ranks of the party up to the eve of the Raid. For a notable instance, Villa's vanguard encountered seventeen cowpunchers at a roundup in Boca Grande on March 7. Villa first proceeded to kill Arthur McKinney, the American foreman. He next ordered that the Mexican hands be made prisoners, whereupon they offered to join up with him. Pleased to take on more raiders, he welcomed them and returned their arms. All of Villa's men then replaced their exhausted mounts with horses from the *remuda*. About noon the camp cook returned and was promptly shot, since Villa had no use for him.[24] With cattle for meat and with fresh horses under his men, the guerrilla could now bear down on Columbus.

Meantime, in the same month of March, General Pershing received the disturbing news at Fort Bliss that Villa planned to attack somewhere north of the Mexican border. The commandant at Juárez confirmed this report from Mexican military intelligence. Pershing would inevitably think of El Paso as Villa's objective. Since September 24, 1915, the American officer had been aware from his own intelligence sources "that if the United States recognized Carranza, Villa planned to attack El Paso with 15,000 men."[25] The garrison at Columbus had received the latest information on Villa's whereabouts. A headline story in the *El Paso Times* on the day before the Raid referred to Palomas, Chihuahua, as the likely target.

> Information received in El Paso last night from the 13th Cavalry, stationed at Columbus, New Mexico, was to the effect that Villa had been sighted 15 miles west of Palomas, Monday night, and was camped there all day Tuesday. What his plans are at this time is not known.

Villa is reported to have between 300 and 400 men with him. They are all well mounted and since arriving near Palomas have been slaughtering large numbers of cattle. There is but a small Carranza garrison at Palomas and it is believed that Villa intends making an attack on the town.[26]

On the morning of March 8, Juan Favela, foreman of the Palomas Land and Cattle Company, hastened to the Army headquarters at Columbus to see the commandant, Herbert J. Slocum. Favela straightway reported that, after topping a hill south of town, he had sighted a large force of riders below him and had immediately recognized the Villistas and their mustached leader. He had come right back, convinced that Colonel Slocum would be interested in his observations. The colonel listened but did not share Favela's fears.

Slocum can hardly be censured for not investigating the ranch foreman's report. The colonel had the task of sifting such reports, and this was not the first one he had heard. Favela's version, in fact, contradicted the account of a presumably trustworthy Mexican informant to the effect that Villa had gone south toward Guzmán.[27]

Yet the veracity of Juan Favela is not open to challenge. On March 7, the day before his observations, intelligence sources communicated to Fort Bliss that Villa's forces (assertedly numbering between 1,000 and 1,500) were camped south of Columbus.[28] Their campsite, located near the Casas Grandes River, was at Boca Grande.

Villa and his band remained in the camp at Boca Grande overnight; that is, until March 8. He had sent Lieutenant Colonel Cipriano Vargas and another officer to Columbus to scout the town and garrison. During their absence, he discussed with his staff the idea of attacking Columbus. He entertained some misgivings because three ranch hands had escaped him when he overran Boca Grande. He feared that they might have alerted the Columbus outpost and spoiled his opportunity for a surprise raid. To satisfy his doubts, he therefore decided to wait for Vargas' report, fresh from the American settlement.[29]

At approximately noon on March 8, Vargas and the other scout returned with their report. They were convinced, presumably, that

Pancho Villa at Columbus [15

there were only about thirty American soldiers on the post. They said that nobody had challenged them or recognized them during their mission. Although the report was encouraging, Villa accepted it in silence. Some of his subordinates, privately opposed to the attack, did not voice their reservations, lest Villa's silence be only a ruse to test their courage. After a long wait, he announced at 2:00 P.M. his consent to the plan for assault.[30] Villa had 485 men in his raiding party — not a number in the thousands, as sometimes reported.[31] At about 4:00 P.M., riders left the river camp and rode northeast toward Columbus in the following formation:

Advance Guard
Colonel Candelario Cervantes . . . . 80 men

Main Body (in order of march)
(a) Colonel Nicolás Fernández . . . . 60 men
(b) General Francisco Villa Hdqrs., Staff and Escort . 80 men
(c) General Pablo López . . . . 100 men
(d) General Juan Pedrosa . . . . 40 men
(e) General Francisco Beltrán . . . . 125 men

485 men

The rear guard consisted of a detachment of ten belonging to Beltrán's band (included in the above total).

This determined group of horsemen continued northward until 1:00 A.M., March 9, when they halted at an arroyo. After further delays, they crossed the international line about two and one-half miles west of the Border Gate, bypassing the outpost there.[32] They rode on slowly and quietly, until the lead guard reached a spot 500 yards south of the railroad tracks and 2,000 yards west of Columbus Knoll. There Villa gave the order to dismount. Then he prepared to execute a difficult military maneuver; namely, converging columns at night. The awesome guerrilla now stood neck deep in the most serious quandary of his life: Should he ride at the head of his men into Columbus or should he designate some of the *Dorados* to lead them?

After deciding to appoint his officers to be the leaders, Villa spoke directly to them:

1. *Cervantes*, you and your men proceed in a line as skirmishers with the knoll [pointing] to your right; occupy it with your detachment. Half of my escort will come to you for whatever instructions and use you decide best.
2. You, *Pablo López*, and your group form a skirmish line on the left of Cervantes. Advance, taking the railroad track as your central guide line.
3. *Fernández*, you form a line of skirmishers facing east to the left of López; attack the Americans from the north.
4. You, *Beltrán*, take your men to form on Fernández's left; you attack also from the north to envelop the Americans.
5. *Pedrosa*, you stay here with the horses and one half of my escort in reserve.
6. I will remain available with the reserve.[33]

It will be noted that Villa's last statement places him behind the lines "with the reserve." This official battle plan, as reproduced in the Pershing Papers, helps to settle one controversial point. There can now be no valid questioning of Villa's presence in Columbus on that fateful Thursday morning.[34] It is also pertinent that several persons saw him there, including Don José Covarrubias, himself one of the raiders, who lives in Juárez today; and Mrs. Maude Hawk Wright (now Mrs. Maude Medders), who had been his prisoner since March 1.[35]

The Surprise Attack

The exact time of the raid has also been a matter for difference of opinion. A photograph[36] of the clock at the Columbus station shows it stopped at exactly 4:11 A.M. The clock was struck by a bullet which put it out of operation. The variations of a few minutes, in the different accounts, can be attributed to the idiosyncracies of timepieces consulted by different eyewitnesses. At approximately 4:15 A.M., then, Villa's band formed in a line of skirmishers facing east. Villa told his men to go ahead, "*Váyanse adelante, muchachos!*" and the attack was on. The countersign was "*Viva México!*"[37]

The dark morning of March 9 enveloped Columbus in a velvet blackness that obscured even the nearest objects. The straggling town of approximately four hundred consisted of a cluster of adobe

Colonel Villa in El Paso in 1912.

Villa in guerrilla dress.

Bullet hole stopped the depot clock at exact time the raid started, 4:11 A.M.

Villa at the head of his troops in early days.

houses, some frame buildings, a railroad station, two hotels, a few other business establishments, and an army camp. Persistent desert winds caused the streets to drift with sand.[38] On this morning, the citizens of Columbus and the soldiers of the 13th Cavalry Regiment slept peacefully, unaware of anything outside except mesquite, cactus, rattlesnakes, and the soundless but ever-moving sand. The main street, Broadway, ran east to west. On it stood J. L. Walker's hardware store, J. T. Dean's grocery store, C. Dewitt Miller's drugstore, the Hoover Hotel, and other business places. The largest enterprise was the Ravel brothers' store. The Commercial Hotel, a two-story frame building owned by Sam Ravel and operated by W. T. Ritchie, was on Taft Street, near the railroad station. A motion-picture theatre stood across the street from the hotel.[39]

Suddenly the rattle of gunfire shattered the desert silence. Private Fred Griffin, the sentinel on post number three at Regimental Headquarters, had challenged a group of Mexicans around Lieutenant Lucas' quarters. The raiders answered his challenge with a fusillade of rifle bullets, mortally wounding him. Before he died, he killed three of the marauders. These shots heralded the general attack. Villistas surged forth, shooting, yelling, and smashing doors and windows. They set fire to Sam Ravel's Commercial Hotel. Provoking complete surprise, the bandits entered the town before anyone knew of their presence. Their battle cry was *"Viva Villa!"* and — allegedly — *"Muerte a los gringos!"*[40]

Then followed the inevitable confusion which accompanies a surprise raid. Officers of the 13th Cavalry were absent. According to regulations, they had locked the arms and ammunition inside the guard house. The startled soldiers had to smash locks to obtain the weapons. In the first moments, it was extremely difficult to identify the enemy; also, the complicated Benet-Mercier machine guns promptly jammed when the sleepy soldiers attempted to fire them.[41] Members of the Sanitary Detachment ("medics"), gripped by panic, barricaded themselves in the hospital and refused to participate in the fight raging outside their bulletproof building. When members of the Machine Gun Troop tried to enter the building to change a broken firing pin — in a place where it would be safe to have a light — the demoralized medical corpsmen refused to let them in.[42]

Some panic-stricken civilians attempted to flee into the desert; others, though frightened and dazed, fought valiantly to protect their homes and places of business. Throughout, the invaders continued their wild fusillade. When Milton James sought to convey his pregnant wife to the relative safety of the Hoover Hotel with its adobe walls, she was struck down by a bullet, to die soon after. During this time, the screams of women and children punctuated the continuous crackle of rifle fire.[43]

The raiders encountered resistance almost immediately from American military personnel, who retaliated as promptly as possible. Lieutenant James P. Castleman, officer of the day on March 8, had found everything so quiet and peaceful during his tour of the camp near midnight that he had gone to the railroad station to greet members of the Regimental polo team, who arrived on the midnight train. Upon returning to his quarters, he had decided to read, instead of going to sleep. At about 4:15 A.M., when preparing to make a final inspection of the guard, he heard the first sound of rifle fire near Regimental Headquarters.

Lieutenant Castleman ran out of the O.D. quarters and straightway encountered one of the Mexican raiders. The raider shot at him point-blank — and missed; the Mexican rifleman was so close, however, that the blast from his weapon almost seared Castleman's face. That proved to be the attacker's last mistake, for the lieutenant killed him with one shot before the Villista could fire again. Then Castleman, heading for the guard tent, crossed the parade ground under heavy enemy fire. Elements of the raiding party seemed to be everywhere, but the American reached the tent safely. Under his direction, the guard then laid down an effective fire. The lieutenant next ran for the line of stables, alerting the detail there, before he continued on to his own unit, Troop F.[44]

Castleman discovered, upon his arrival, that Sergeant Michael Fody had already turned out the troop and armed its components. Castleman thereupon deployed the troop in order to concentrate fire on the raiders' right flank. Other troopers, whose commanders remained trapped in Columbus, armed themselves to join Lt. Castleman's group. Under their combined fire, the American troopers slowly forced the Mexican aggressors backward. At first the Americans fired with hesitance, for fear of shooting their own comrades. But when they heard Mexicans shouting in Spanish in front of them, they energetically laid down a withering fire on the enemy. The troopers soon advanced, in the face of heavy opposition, to Regimental Headquarters and drove the enemy from that position. Thereupon Castleman, after stationing a small detail on guard, began a cautious advance toward Columbus. His purpose was to protect the officers' families by expelling the invaders from the residential areas. The troopers circled to the right, advancing along the railroad track.

Castleman's men made several "stands" in flanking their way around the business section. The troopers first pushed rapidly forward to a point where they could take advantage of cover. From this point, they fired from kneeling or prone positions until a lull in the enemy's fire permitted another advance. Private Thomas Butler sustained a wound on the second stand but kept firing until he had been wounded four more times, the last wound being fatal. The raiders attempted to hold a point near the railroad track, but the relentless fire of the troopers drove them away. Many of the marauding Mexicans died in this fight. Castleman's riflemen, after battling their way into town from the east, took a position on the main street near the bank, firing up and down the street with telling effect. The American line now faced west, with the right flank in front of Castleman's house and the left in front of the bank. This strategy diverted some of the Mexican attackers from the military installations; it also protected a portion of the business district and gave Castleman command of the town's main artery. By this time, the Commercial Hotel had burst into roaring flames, illuminating the raiders clearly.[45]

While troopers under Lieutenant Castleman drove through the eastern section of Columbus, Lieutenant John Lucas and the Machine Gun Troop put their balky machines into action. The

Villistas, at this time, found themselves in a crossfire — crouching, their figures silhouetted by burning buildings. The fight had developed into something more than they had expected. At about 5:30 A.M., Colonel Slocum arrived. He ordered Castleman, who already had distinguished himself in the defense, to hold the town on the east at any cost. As it was now past dawn and as the raiders had met with unexpectedly stiff resistance, their attack began to slacken and disintegrate. Here and there a few minor skirmishes occurred before the Villistas withdrew in full retreat.

The American Defense

Under the conditions of Pancho Villa's sudden dawn attack, or *albazo*, the effective resistance of the surprised and outnumbered American military personnel at Columbus seems worthy of recognition. Historians in both the Southwest and Mexico have nonetheless critized in particular the officers assigned to the Columbus garrison. Dr. I. J. Bush, a Southwestern writer, regards the American defense as a fiasco and credits a report that the absent commanding officer, Slocum, was drunk: "It is claimed that nearly all the officers were attending a dance at Deming, and that the Colonel in Command was incapacitated as the result of a prolonged session with Mr. John Barleycorn the evening before."[46] Alberto Salinas Carranza, a Mexican historian, charges Major Frank Tompkins with cowardice. In spite of the fact that the raiders isolated and encircled Tompkins, preventing him from joining his command amid the heaviest fighting, Salinas Carranza accuses the American major of having "*corvas*" or "cold feet."[47]

One of the staunchest defenders at the army camp was Lieutenant John P. Lucas, who figured vitally in the fray. After visiting in El Paso on March 8 with the Regimental polo team, he had returned on the midnight train, the so-called "Drummers'" or "Drunkards'" Special. When he reached his quarters early on March 9, he discovered that the shells had been taken out of his revolver by his roommate, Lt. C. C. Benson. Lucas had to move several boxes to get ammunition from his trunk to reload. He later remarked that ordinarily he would not have taken the trouble to reload, and attributed his doing so to a "hunch."[48]

Lt. Lucas then went to sleep but soon was awakened by riders passing the open window of his room. Looking out, he recognized them as foraying Mexicans by their steeple-crowned sombreros. Quickly he dressed and grasped his loaded pistol, ready to sell his life dearly — for the house was completely surrounded. In the dark, he could not find his boots and dared not strike a light. Outside the barracks, Private Griffin, the sentry at Regimental Headquarters, probably saved Lucas' life when Griffin challenged the advancing Villistas. For reply, the raiders charged the sentry and killed him.

Lucas, still barefoot, dashed out of his room and raced to his unit, the Machine Gun Troop, where he found the acting first sergeant turning out his men. Lucas next rushed toward the Mexicans who were firing upon the tent which housed the machine guns. Private J. D. Yarborough, with his right arm now shattered by a bullet, stood guarding the guns. Though seriously wounded, Yarborough operated his pistol with his left hand, helping to hold off the attackers. He later lost his right arm because of the severity of this wound.[49]

When the American machine guns went into action, thirty riflemen came running up to report to Lucas. He deployed them along the railroad line, to fire on the raiders in town. He next ordered Lieutenant Horace Stringfellow, who had just arrived, to take several men to protect their left flank from further attacks from the west. After these defensive measures, Lucas turned the troop over to Captain Hamilton Bowie, who had just arrived. Lucas then took some men and with them worked his way across the tracks into town, finding Castleman and his troopers already there. It was now nearly daylight.

Colonel Slocum arrived about this time. He sent Lucas, with a small detachment, to relieve Captain Jens E. Stedje at the Border Gate, so that Stedje could join in the pursuit of the Villistas. Slocum, the commanding officer, quickly grasped the dangers in

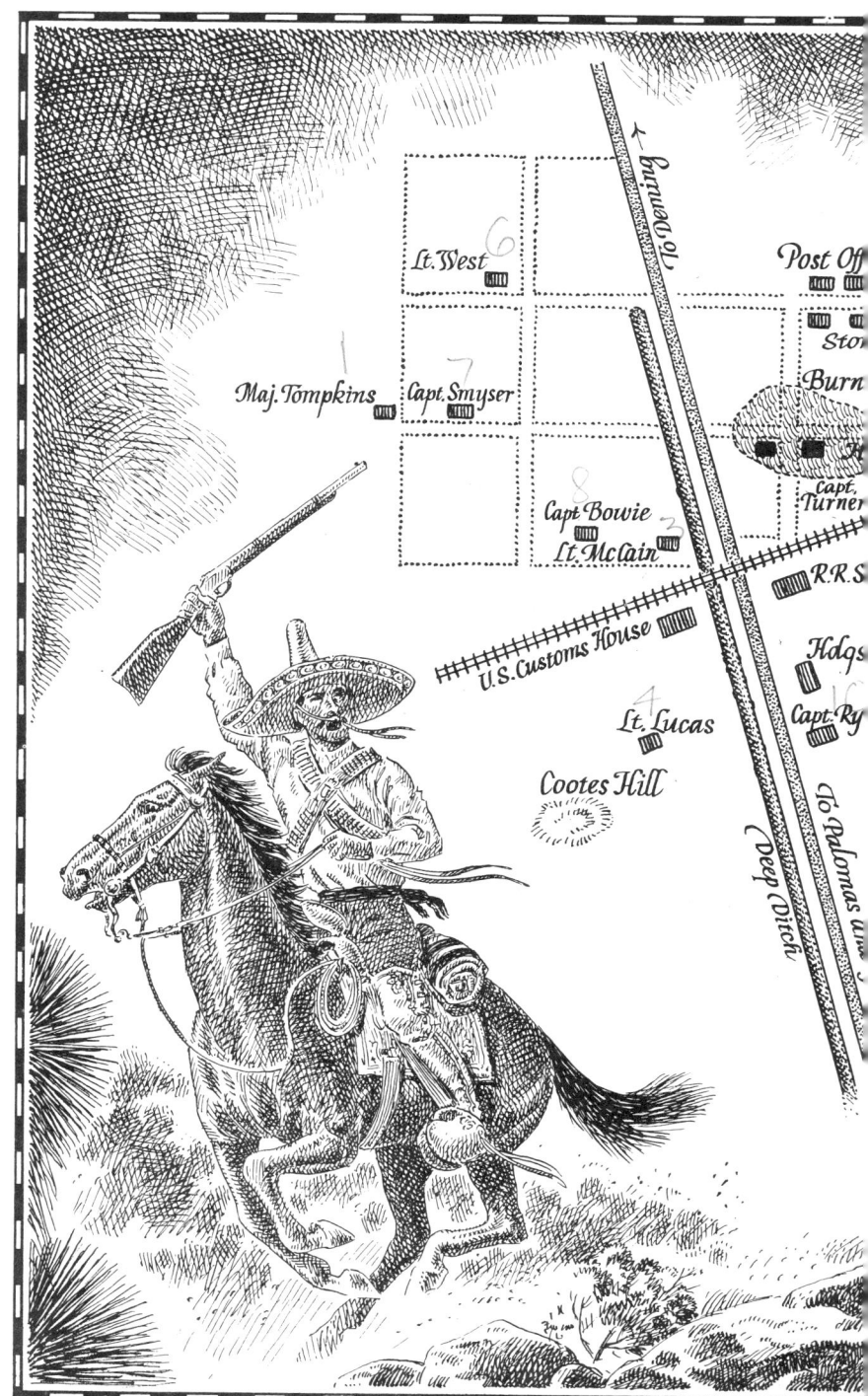

the situation, and issued orders that repulsed the enemy. Tompkins participated in the rout of the invaders and even undertook, as will be seen later, the responsibility of crossing over into Mexico to chase the fleeing guerrillas.

The bravery of both officers and soldiers at the Columbus camp blunted the force of Villa's attack. Their courage in fighting and dying there prevented a complete sack of the town and military camp. Had the military made no defense and permitted the attackers to overrun them, the Columbus affair might have ended quite seriously. Instead of being a fragment of recent American history, it might have become a milestone of guerrilla rapine.

Castleman and Lucas survived the guerrilla assault as the heroic leaders of the military garrison. Castleman, as already narrated, discovered that the Villistas were startled by the promptness of the American resistance. In the fight, he made the most of their dismay. Lucas, looking back later on the raid, remarked that the Mexicans were either poor shots or were nervous. He said that "One of them fired at me with a rifle. . . . He missed me even though he was so close that I easily killed him with a revolver and I was never noted for my excellence in pistol practice."[50]

The incidents as chronicled by Tompkins, Castleman, and Lucas comprise substantially what happened at the assaulted army camp.

In the town of Columbus itself, the Villistas appeared bent on finding Sam Ravel. After all, he and his brothers operated the leading mercantile store. Besides this, the raiders were familiar with the location of this well-stocked store, reportedly having traded with the Ravels. American civilian survivors of the Columbus Raid are in agreement that Villa himself seemed to have a personal grudge against these prosperous merchants — in particular against Sam, the eldest brother. According to rumor, he and Villa had experienced violent differences of a personal nature.

At any rate, on this early morning Arthur Ravel, a youth of fourteen, and his elder brother, Louis, were sleeping in the back room of their store. Raiders started pounding on the door and forced it open. Art faced them after they broke in. They first demanded to see Sam. Failing in this, they then demanded the combination to the safe, but the lad told them that he did not know it. He later said, "I honestly can't remember now if I knew the combination to the safe or not."[51] Villa's minions fired several shots into the door of the safe in an attempt to force it open. Not succeeding in this, two of them dragged him outside, the others following. They took him to the Commercial Hotel because they thought that Sam Ravel, the owner of the building, might be hiding there. But Sam at this time was in a hospital in El Paso, undergoing minor surgery.

The invaders had the Commercial surrounded when Art and his captors arrived. Ten or fifteen of them rushed inside and dragged out three men and a woman. They killed the three men — and apparently intended to shoot the woman. When she cried, "*Viva México!*" they lowered their guns, letting her go free. Then the two captors started back to the store, holding the boy firmly by the arms between them. Just before they reached the store, gunfire felled both Villistas, leaving Art free and unharmed. Still in his underwear, he raced away, running three miles before stopping.[52]

As the confusion mounted and spread to wider areas, several other incidents involved military personnel as well as civilians. These anecdotal episodes range from the heroic to the ludicrous.

The soldiers' barracks were wooden buildings; the stables for the horses, merely open sheds. The army kitchens, however, were relatively bulletproof, being constructed of thick adobe. As the fighting spread, some of the Mexican raiders broke into a kitchen. The startled cooks, already up preparing breakfast, met them with whatever weapons they had or could improvise. One cook poured boiling water on the attackers; a second cook killed a Villista with an axe.

The kitchen detail kept shotguns to be used in supplementing their regular rations with the small game that abounded in the desert near camp. The Americans grabbed these guns and used them so effectively that their attackers withdrew.[53] In their turn, members of the stable detail had no opportunity to arm themselves in the early moments of the fight. But they shortly were able to fight back, too. In the melee one member of the detail managed to kill a raider with a baseball bat.[54]

Back in Columbus, Steve Birchfield, a civilian, was dragged from his room in the Commercial Hotel, searched, and robbed of all his cash. The Mexicans showed their displeasure at the small return by threatening to shoot him. He said, "Now boys — *muchachos* . . . That's all the cash I have on me, but I do have my checkbook here. I'll just write out what you want."[55] He asked them to line up to get the checks, which he began to write with a flourish. Then it dawned on the raiders that taking checks under these conditions might not be very sensible. They wanted to know how they could trust the *americano*. Fortunately, at this time, he recognized Eligio Hernández among the raiders and nodded to him a warning. Birchfield had helped him evade the American authorities after Hernández had killed a woman by the name of Ponce. The fugitive subsequently had slipped over into Mexico, now to reappear as a Villista under an assumed name. Hernández stepped forth and said: "His check is good. I will personally guarantee any check he writes."[56] Birchfield thereupon wrote them all the checks they wanted, and they spared his life.

It proved a rather lucky night for another civilian resident: the Ravel brother, Louis. When the raid began, he hid under a stack of cowhides. The invaders tore down the stack looking for hidden valuables but upon finding nothing, stopped with the last few hides. Louis Ravel was under the last hide.[57]

Jess Fuller, a civilian official, had luck too. He crouched behind a rain barrel for protection. When a bullet struck the barrel, Fuller believed he had been shot to death, for he could feel something moist trickling down his shirt. The "blood" of course turned out to be water; and in this manner Fuller escaped with no more than a bad scare.[58]

The Women at Columbus

Throughout the hasty defense, the mothers in the town and the wives of military men at the post displayed the hardy pioneer spirit of the frontier. When the raid started, A. B. Frost, a citizen of Columbus, placed his wife and their three-months-old baby in their automobile and backed it out of the garage in a move to escape the developing gun battle. A shot struck him before he could get very far. Just after taking the road for Deming, he suffered a second wound and found himself unable to continue driving. It was then that Mrs. Frost moved her husband to the back seat of the car and drove the family to safety in Deming.[59]

At the army camp, when the invaders battered in the front door, Captain Rudolph E. Smyser, his wife, and two children climbed out a window and hid in an outhouse. The Mexicans, frustrated at not finding them, talked of searching the place. Overhearing this, the Smysers quit the outhouse to hide in the desert. In their flight they were cut and scratched by cactus thorns; but they were otherwise unharmed when Major Tompkins found them soon afterward. Captain Smyser immediately bade his family goodbye and joined Tompkin's cavalrymen in the pursuit of the fleeing Villistas.[60]

On the night of the raid, Captain Thomas F. Ryan was assigned to patrol duty at Gibson's Ranch. Mrs. Ryan, at home alone, realized that their adobe garage would give her protection from gunfire, whereas their frame house could not. While making for the safety of the garage, she was seized by a Villista. He asked where she was going, "*Adónde va?*" To this she replied, "Nowhere." With no more ado, he released her.[61]

After the raid began, Lieutenant William A. McCain and an orderly moved the McCain family out of their west-side home. They headed south, crossed the railroad tracks, and found refuge in the mesquite. McCain and his orderly between them had only a pistol and a shotgun. When one lone marauder chanced upon them, they fired at him with the shotgun but merely wounded him. When they tried to finish him off with a knife, to prevent his outcries from revealing their location, the blade proved to be too dull. The two Americans finally had to kill him by battering him with the butt of the pistol. Although only a few feet away, Mrs. McCain and her daughter stifled any outcry and kept their emotions in check throughout the fatal beating.[62]

At the outbreak of the hostilities, Lee Riggs, the deputy customs collector, put his family on the floor and lined mattresses against the walls for their protection. Fearing that the cries of their five-months-old baby would betray their whereabouts, Mrs. Riggs stuffed a pillowcase into the baby's mouth; she held it there as long as she dared, until the baby became limp. Fortunately, by this time, the firing had so diminished that she was able to remove the gag and let the baby catch its breath.[63]

About a mile south of Columbus, Major Tompkins found Mrs. J. J. Moore in distress. Though crippled by a painful leg wound, she had managed to crawl into the safety of a mesquite clump. Her husband had been murdered and their house set afire. Mrs. Moore was cared for by Mrs. Wright, who had just been set free by Villa near there.[64]

Of all the instances of courage among the women at Columbus, Mrs. Maud Hawk Wright's experiences stand out most memorably. She had been captured at her ranch near Pearson, Chihuahua. On March 1, 1916, Candelario Cervantes with a pack of foraging Villistas stripped her house of everything edible and stole thirteen horses from the ranch. They also bound and took prisoner her husband, Edward John Wright, as well as his assistant at the La Booker Sawmill, Frank Hayden. Cervantes' men made her leave her baby behind but carried the mother off as a captive. Preparatory to rejoining Villa, they placed her on a mule and forced her to make the difficult journey northward, in ignorance of the fate of either her husband or her baby.[65] She did not learn that her baby was still alive but that her husband had been murdered until the day after the Columbus Raid, March 10.[66]

Throughout the grueling journey toward the United States line, Mrs. Wright slept on the desert sand, with nothing to eat but a little half-cooked mule meat. Villa remarked during her ordeal that since she could withstand hunger and exposure better than his own *muchachos,* he would rather let her die of exhaustion than kill her outright. When one of Villa's *jefes* taunted her by saying that he would give her a rifle and make her fire on the Americans at Columbus, she told him that if he gave her a rifle he would be

Columbus, New Mexico, a few days before the raid. Compare next page.
(Courtesy Aultman Collection)

Columbus the day after the raid — same street as shown on previous page.
(Courtesy Bill McGaw)

Pancho Villa at Columbus [29

her first target.[67] The Negro prisoner "Bunk" Spencer, taken captive before she was, is reported in a newspaper of March 15, 1916, as saying: "She is the gamest woman God ever let live."[68] He explained her bravery as the only reason why the Villistas did not mistreat her.

It was near the Moores' home that Mrs. Wright won her release. In answer to her plea for freedom, Villa, who had come to admire her courage, told her to go, that she was at liberty: *"Puedes irte; estás libre."*[69] After being set free, the valiant lady assisted in caring for Mrs. Moore and other wounded Americans. Finally, Colonel Slocum's wife took Mrs. Wright over, put her to bed, and gave her the first full meal that she had eaten in nine days.[70] Afterward she was told that her baby was safe at Pearson but that there were no practical means for her to get there. The woman of indomitable spirit replied: "I want to go to my baby; it would only take me three days to walk to Pearson."[71]

Following the bloodshed, American casualties were totaled. The raid had cost the Americans eighteen lives: ten civilians (including one woman) and eight soldiers. Four soldiers, two officers, and two civilians had been wounded. A list of eighteen killed and eight wounded follows:

Civilians and Soldiers Killed

Pvt. Thomas Butler	C. C. Miller
W. A. Davidson	Charles DeWitt Miller
Harry Davis	J. J. Moore
James Dean	Sgt. John G. Nievergelt
Sgt. Mark A. Dobbs	William T. Ritchie
Pvt. Fred Griffin	Corp. Paul Simon
Dr. H. M. Hart	Pvt. Jesse P. Taylor
Mrs. Milton James	John Walton Walker
Pvt. Frank T. Kindval	Corp. Harry A. Wiswell

Civilians and Soldiers Wounded

Corp. Michael Barmazel	Mrs. J. J. Moore
Lt. Clarence C. Benson	Pvt. James Venner
Milton James	Capt. George Williams
Pvt. Theodore Katzorke	Pvt. John D. Yarborough[72]

As for the Mexican dead: ninety Villistas were killed during the raid on Columbus. This number includes those who subsequently died of their wounds. Twenty-three raiders suffered less serious wounds. A smaller number of Mexicans were taken prisoner.[73]

The morning after the raid, a detail of American cavalrymen used cordwood and coal oil to cremate their dead horses. Forty of their mounts had been shot in the raid. They then piled the bodies of the dead Villistas in another lot, similarly cremating them.

The element of tragedy and savagery at Columbus was hardly one-sided. As for American deaths, the needless murder of unarmed John Walton Walker made his bride of twenty-eight days a heartbroken widow. He was torn from her arms and shot to death on the stairs of the Commercial Hotel. As for the aggressors, one of their leaders later that morning lay in the dirt, seriously wounded but still alive. When Colonel Slocum saw him lying there, he reportedly said, "Let him bake in the sun." It is further reported that one of the Americans gathering up the cadavers hit the wounded man in the head and threw him, still alive, into a wagon conveying bodies to the makeshift crematory.[74]

Retreat of the Villistas

At daylight, after discovering the strength of the American forces to be much greater than Villa's scout Vargas had reported, the guerrillas began to retreat. They did so in a semblance of order. The withdrawal started with a few riders carrying their wounded to the reserve where the horses stood tethered. Then individual Mexicans straggled southward, along with the wounded and those supporting them. Finally, whole groups of mounted men began to retire.[75]

All of the raiders except Cervantes, Fernández, and a small group had withdrawn by 7:15 A.M. Cervantes joined them at 7:30 A.M., completing the withdrawal. Villa and about thirty riflemen remained on a hill southeast of town to cover the retreat.[76]

The reserve area was a shallow gulch in Columbus behind an embankment. Adhering to his plan, Villa had stayed here to guard their horses. Jesús Paiz, a twelve-year-old lad, had also remained behind to help. Captured after the foray, the boy attested to these facts. Mrs. Wright recounted that when the retreaters reached this area, "Villa rode among them, cursing and threatening any man who ran away, but they kept going back."[77] Villa's own directions to his lieutenants which placed him with the reserve are thus corroborated by both a Mexican witness and an American captive. This body of evidence supersedes the undocumented accounts which located the raider chief "in the center" of the fighting;[78] it definitively limits the role of Villa himself at Columbus. He came in person to that *pueblito*. In response to a recent query (March 21, 1962), Mrs. Wright wrote: "Yes, I saw Villa enter Columbus." But it would be contrary to the authentic documents and witnesses cited here ever to hold that Villa himself reached the focus of the action.

There remains another well-authenticated incident. This involved "Bunk" Spencer, an American Negro, already mentioned as Mrs. Wright's fellow prisoner. Before his capture, he had been an employee of the E. K. Warren and Sons' Ranch, El Salto de Agua, Chihuahua. The Villistas had held him prisoner since late February. They had seized him when the Villista José Ynez Salazar and a number of *compañeros* plundered the ranch buildings and property where Spencer worked. Upon arriving in Columbus, the Villistas turned him over to the rear guard holding the horses. When bullets began flying in this area during the Mexican retreat, Spencer told the guard that the action was getting too hot and that they should be on the move. The guard then told him that he could go — that he was free. He departed the area with all speed but fled west from Columbus, for fear of being mistaken for a Villista. Daylight found him making for Hachita, a few miles away.[79]

The full light of day revealed the extent of havoc wreaked on Columbus. The burned area, covering less than a block, had at its center Sam Ravel's edifice, the Commercial Hotel. In this area, buildings still smoldered. The dead had not yet been cleared from the streets, and many of the wounded yet demanded immediate care. But it was the military area which bore the brunt of pillage.

Official records describe in detail the quantity of food and supplies that the raiders purportedly carried away from the post. Reported missing were eighty fine-bred American horses, thirty mules, a considerable assortment of military equipment, including some three-hundred Mausers.[80] Abortive as the Columbus Raid was, Pancho Villa still succeeded in terms of booty.

As the sun rose higher, a group of soldiers directed by Colonel Slocum focused their fire on the retiring raiders from a position on Cootes Hill.[81] While Slocum's soldiers kept firing from the west, Major Tompkins and his men rode out of Columbus and headed for Mexico. Immediately, Captain Smyser joined in the pursuit with his Troop H.[82] On the outskirts of town Captain George Williams also met and joined them. About three-hundred yards south of the boundary, a body of Villa's troops covered the escape from the vantage point of a hill. With marked courage, Tompkins and his party galloped southward with pistols drawn, gradually increasing their speed. The Villistas, ready on their hill, opened fire on their pursuers; but the shots came too high and inaccurately to repulse the pursuers. The withdrawing raiders held their positions until the cavalrymen reached the lower slope, whereupon they broke and ran. Continuing to the top of the hill, the cavalrymen then holstered their pistols, dismounted, and fired their rifles at the fleeing guerrillas.[83]

Hesitating to violate the Mexican boundary further, Major Tompkins halted his advance and sent a courier back to Columbus for authority to continue the pursuit. While Tompkins awaited reply, Lieutenant Castleman arrived with Troop F, consisting of twenty-seven men. Forty-five minutes later Colonel Slocum answered by authorizing Tompkins to use his own judgment.[84] The Major judged the occasion fitting to push on.

Troops F and H thereupon moved rapidly in the wake of the fleeing *hombres montados*,[85] who had been firing intermittently and inaccurately. After approaching the Mexican rear guard, the Americans drove it back to its main column with their rifle fire. The cavalrymen were able to continue the pursuit at such a rapid pace that they soon overtook the entire body of raiders. In trying

Pancho Villa at Columbus [33

to turn the left flank of the Mexicans, the Americans unfortunately exposed themselves to heavy enemy fire. At this time, Major Tompkins received a slight wound in the knee; Captain Williams, a minor one in the hand. To avoid the concentrated Mexican gunfire, the troopers dismounted for a better aim at the enemy. Both Troops F and H simultaneously poured a punishing fire into the remaining body of the raiders, driving them deeper into Mexico. Again the cavalrymen resumed the chase, but at this stage the Mexicans assembled at a vantage point. When they took time to observe how small the pursuing force was, the Villistas regrouped to launch a counter-attack with about three hundred men. Greatly outnumbered, Tompkins withdrew four hundred yards to prepare for the expected assault.[86]

After waiting three quarters of an hour for the counterattack to materialize, Major Tompkins decided to return to the army headquarters. His ammunition was running low; a hot morning of fighting without food or water had exhausted both his men and their mounts.[87]

Villa effected a successful escape, but at a relatively high price. He escaped personally untouched;[88] well over a hundred of his *muchachos*, however, lay dead.[89] He lost a good deal of the material and food he had pillaged at Columbus, as well as two prized machine guns and a substantial amount of small arms and ammunition.[90] He also lost to his pursuers an uncounted number of horses; this loss was the most galling of all.

Horses had always been the key to Villa's lightning mobility. Pancho Villa indulged a military veteran's weakness for combat, wine and women — but his overriding passion was for fine horseflesh. He won for himself early in the Revolution the title *Centauro del Norte*. The adventurer-writer John Reed, who knew Villa personally, once said that "The movements of his feet and legs are awkward — he always rode a horse."[91]

The fact is that Villa prized good horses. A number of those he owned live on in legend to illuminate his prowess as "The Centaur of the North." They include the famous roan *Taurino*, probably his mount at Columbus; and the most celebrated of all, the white horse *Siete Leguas* (Seven Leagues). Most Americans wrongly claim that he rode a white horse on the Raid.

A handsome steed was one of the few things that Villa would pay for, not merely appropriate. Years earlier, he paid $200 in cash for the prize stud *Príncipe Tirano* (Prince Tyrant). Butch Cassidy, acting for the owner, George A. Brown, made the deal.[92] Prince Tyrant was a black stallion with a white flag on his forehead.

Now, the American cavalry had developed a durable strain from crossbreeding with pure Arabian stock, adapted to patrolling desert terrain. These hybrid animals had the speed and stamina of the Arabian together with the size and ruggedness of the American packhorse. As an isolated outpost, Columbus had a reserve of such mounts.

On March 9, 1916, there were more horses at Columbus than defenders, a part of the garrison then being off post, including the commanding officer. These circumstances made the little frontier outpost a more attractive site for a guerrilla operation than, say, Fort Bliss. Had Villa been thinking in terms of vengefully inflicting casualties, Fort Bliss would have become his objective. The New Mexico incursion is adequately explained as guerrilla foraging.[93]

The driving passion of the Villistas was their need — the unremitting need of money, clothes, arms, ammunition, and, as mainstay of their profession, horseflesh. Money and clothes from *ricos* like rich Sam Ravel — and from the *militares*, arms, ammunition, and horses!

The Outcome Appraised

After the Raid the wildest kinds of rumors seized the American imagination. Many people, knowing little about politics in Mexico, associated this invasion of the United States with the Mexican government. Others interpreted it as inspired by the German government to prevent America from joining the Allied Powers in World War I.[94] A minority theorized that the United States government itself had clandestinely arranged for the Raid in order to whip up war sentiment and to use Mexican soil for tactical maneuvers.[95]

Actually, neither the American nor the Mexican government can be proved responsible for the Columbus Raid by either furnishing funds or divulging military data to Villa.

The United States, with its citizens already sympathetic with the Allies, stood to lose more than it could possibly gain by so risky a tactic. There were, however, American investors residing in Mexico who would have welcomed intervention by their government to protect their interests and prevent further despoliation.[96] But the State Department would have been reckless indeed if it had sought to involve the United States in a war with the Carranza regime. Maneuvers on this scale could hardly be kept secret for long and would have produced a disastrous revulsion of public sentiment.

German Intelligence of the time would have appreciated the tactical value of estranging the two neighbor countries. The Germany of that era would have had everything to gain and nothing to lose by provoking conflict. It is a fact that Villa acquired arms and munitions of German manufacture; he even may have accepted funds from German agents.[97] As a guerrilla, he could not afford to decline aid from any source; also, as a guerrilla, he would not feel formally bound to respect any terms of commitment. In point of fact, the only documented overtures to Mexico from the Imperial German Government came after the Columbus Raid, on January 19, 1917;[98] and these were addressed, not to the proscribed[99] Conventionist bellwether Villa, but to the Constitutionalist President Carranza.

Did the Mexican government instigate the sortie to draw the Americans into their dismembered land?[100] The *de facto* regime had already won the favor and support of the United States. The only disaffected Revolutionary likely to have adopted such strategy would be the raider himself. Villa as the arch-rebel certainly wanted to demonstrate to the Americans the ineffectuality of the *de facto* Carranza government. He may also have reasoned that the native masses again would rally to his standard if the hated *gringos* invaded Mexico in reprisal. Or he may have hoped to lure the United States south to embroil it with the Carrancista regime and thus play off the *gringos* against the *pelones*[101] in double vengeance. Whatever his reasoning, American diplomacy of the time, by siding with Carranza and abetting his operations,[102] had aroused Villa's justified resentment.

No constituted government can be conceived as the author of such a small-scale invasion as the Columbus Raid. In the Southwest the logical military objectives of a foreign power would be the strategically important Fort Bliss at El Paso. Yet Fort Bliss, for all its strategic value, was not an ideal objective for a guerrilla assault. Its location made it difficult to approach without putting its strong garrison on notice. But Columbus stood isolated and sparsely guarded, yet amply supplied in this isolation with reserves of food and arms. This plum of the New Mexico desert lay susceptible to a surprise attack — ripe for the plucking by hungering guerrillas.

Pancho Villa did not ride to Columbus for carnage — but for booty.[103] This he got, but not so totally as planned — because he met with unexpectedly spirited resistance from the heroic defenders. He did not vengefully descend upon Columbus to massacre *gringos*.[104] Villa could have inflicted many more casualties in the time he used to attack Columbus — approximately two hours[105] — during which he killed some eighteen Americans while ransacking the straggling town and its nearby well-fortified military section. The Villistas concentrated on the hotels, whose guests were stripped of cash and valuables, and on well-stocked stores, which they hastily looted. They ignored mainly individual residences, particularly the humble homes of Latin-American citizens deemed as unworthy of pillaging. Eager for plunder, the Villistas had little time for the noncombatants. The looters were occupied with removing horses and conveying available arms and ammunition, which in most instances they encountered either guarded or locked up. Thus the small number of killings, deplorable as they were, occurred more or less incidental to a genuine guerrilla operation.[106]

The raiders spared the solitary fleeing women they found; set free the captives they had. No instances of rape took place; nobody was kidnapped to be held for ransom. If Villa came "*a matar gringos,*" then his raid was virtually a failure.

When the evidence so plainly points to a simple explanation, no purpose is served in either resurrecting outworn theories or creating new speculations to supplant them. The Punitive Expedition into Mexico resulted, not from the Columbus Raid alone, but from this isolated incident as climaxing a series of border outrages. The Raid did constitute the turning point in the tension between the two nations at that time (1910-1916) and brought the American general, Pershing, unprecedentedly onto sovereign Mexican territory in reprisal. Why Villa recklessly violated American territory on March 9, 1916, is no "insoluble mystery."[107] All that happened at Columbus can be satisfactorily explained as inevitable aggression. The Raid distinguished Villa as the unparalleled Mexican guerrilla.[108]

REFERENCES

1. The author wishes to express his gratitude to the Organized Research Fund, Texas Western College, whose aid enabled him to travel in Mexico and to study in Washington, D. C., as well as to employ an Assistant, Mr. Richard Escontrias. Parts of the research cover some thirty years, so that it is impossible to name all of those who aided in the investigation; however, besides those cited in the notes, it seems fitting to mention Mr. Steve Bell, Mrs. Frances Milchen Brown, Mr. Will Burgie, Dr. S. D. Myres, Dr. C. L. Sonnichsen, and Sgt. Arnold N. Sparks.
2. *Pershing Papers,* Box 373 (Library of Congress, Division of Manuscripts). Provocations occurred as early as October 13, 1912, when Mr. John T. Cameron was taken from a train south of El Paso in the heart of the Villa preserve (*William H. Taft Papers,* Presidential Series No. 2, File 3898 [Library of Congress, Division of Manuscripts]).
3. "Wanderers: Mexican Mennonites," *Time,* April 8, 1957.
4. Informant: "Captain" H. D. Slater, now deceased. Mr. Slater was formerly editor of the El Paso *Herald* and then of the *Times.*
5. C. Whitney, *What's the Matter with Mexico?* (New York, 1916), 173.
6. Salvador Caballero B., *Chihuahua en su CCL Aniversario* (Chihuahua City, Mexico, 1960), 183.
7. On the "Golden Ones," see Rito E. Rodríguez, "Como Nació el Nombre de 'Los Dorados de Villa,'" *El Legionario* (August 15, 1957), VII, 18-19. On the Mexican boys participating in the Raid, see Dr. Stivison in footnote 104.
8. *Pershing Papers,* Box 373.
9. "Data Relative to a Part of the Criminal Life of Francisco Villa," *Pershing Papers,* Box 372. There is also a typed copy of this anonymous short document in *Mexican Claims Case Files* (National Archives).
10. Villa was paid $25,000 in cash and $5,000 in supplies for the ransom of Elias Knotts (Informant: Mrs. E. F. Knotts, El Paso, Texas).
11. The Santa Isabel Massacre has been often described. For relevant materials, see the Southwestern Collection, El Paso Public Library.
12. Informant: Mr. Joe Miller, El Paso, Texas. Mr. Miller was personally acquainted with Villa and a number of his men.
13. *Foreign Relations of the United States for 1916* (Washington, D. C., 1925), 465; hereafter, *For. Rel.*
14. Informant: Major H. W. Conklin (U.S.A., Ret.), El Paso, Texas.
15. Clarence C. Clendenen, *The United States and Pancho Villa* (Ithaca, N. Y., 1961), 227.
16. Informant: Major General John L. Hines (U.S.A., Ret.), Chevy Chase, Maryland. The New York *Times* reported on October 26, 1916, that the Republicans had plotted an attack on American forces somewhere on the Mexican border to create sentiment against President Wilson in his candidacy as a Democrat for reelection (*Pershing Papers,* Box 385). For the theory that Wilson and his Cabinet "hired Villa . . .," see Larry A. Harris, *Pancho Villa and the Columbus Raid* (El Paso, Texas, 1949), 94. Some informants (Herman Dawson Camp, El Paso, Texas; Robert N. Mullin, South Laguna, California, *et al.*) reported that American investors in Mexico induced Villa to raid Columbus. For the hypothesis that American undercover agents bribed Villa, see Bill McGaw, "Was Pancho Villa Paid $80,000 for making Raid on Columbus?" *The Southwesterner* (May, 1964), 1, 4-6; see refutation of such ideas in Haldeen Braddy, "Myths of Pershing's Mexican Campaign," *Southern Folklore Quarterly* (September, 1963), XXVII, 181-195.
17. Informant: Don José Covarrubias, Juárez, Chihuahua, as translated from his Spanish.
18. Bill McGaw, "Out of the West," El Paso *Herald-Post,* June 24, 1961.

Pancho Villa at Columbus [39

19. *Ibid.* On United States permission to Carranza to use the American railways for transporting Mexican troops and the intervention by *"expertos americanos a manejar los reflectores . . .,"* see Nellie Campobello, *Apuntes sobre la vida militar de Francisco Villa* (Mexico, D. F., 1940), 117. On Americans also intervening in Naco, Sonora, see Timothy G. Turner, *Bullets, Bottles, and Gardenias* (Dallas, Texas, 1935), 212-214.
20. *For. Rel., 1916*, 480.
21. Miguel V. and Gustavo Casasola, *Historia Gráfica de la Revolución* (2nd ed., México, D. F., n.d.), III, 1022.
22. Hugh Lenox Scott, *Some Memories of a Soldier* (New York, 1928), 517.
23. Tom Mahoney, "The Columbus Raid," *Southwest Review* (1932), XVII, 161. An unpublished list of reasons has been carefully compiled by Miss Bettye Lacy, a former student of Texas Western College. One rumor says that Villa went to Columbus to board a train for Washington, D. C., where he intended to confer with President Wilson. Another reports him crossing to the New Mexico side for the purpose of confining his troops there and surrendering to Colonel Slocum. And yet another has him crossing the division line in order to proceed to California and settle there — or, perhaps, in order to go to Havana, Cuba, to rejoin his legal wife, Sra. Luz Corral de Villa, whom he had already sent there.
24. Bill McGaw, "Out of the West," *El Paso Herald-Post*, February 25, 1961.
25. *Pershing Papers*, Box 373.
26. "Villa Expected to Attack Palomas," *El Paso Times*, March 8, 1916. The fact that the American Associated Press representative, George L. Seese, tried "to obtain the services of a special telegraph operator at Columbus only a few hours before the raid" is hardly a matter for "curiosity" (Clendenen, *op. cit.*, 246) but appears a sensible precautionary attempt under the circumstances. Actually, there had been official warning that Villa was moving toward Columbus as early as March 3 (*For. Rel., 1916*, 478). Moreover, Seese purportedly had received inside data at Juárez from the officer there in command, General Gabriel Gavira, and at Columbus from a defecting Villista.
27. Mr. Juan Favela, who reported to Slocum on Villa's movements, still resides in Columbus, New Mexico. On March 6, 1916, General Gavira publicly advised the American authorities of Villa's approach, so that they might prevent a violation of the boundary (Randolph W. Smith, *Benighted Mexico* [New York, 1916], 344). But the next day the Carranza commander at the Border Gate near Palomas reported to Colonel Slocum that Villa was nowhere near (Dorothy Jean Jackson, *Pershing's Expedition into Mexico* [unpublished University of Texas M.A. Thesis, Austin, 1940], 29). As the American garrison had no orders to advance against Villa, Slocum had no choice except to continue to post sentries, which he did. A railroad section foreman observed nothing unusual on March 9 when he returned to his home in Columbus at 1:00 A.M. after extinguishing a grass fire on the railroad tracks east of town (Tom Mahoney, "When Villa Raided New Mexico," *American Legion Magazine* [1964], LXXVII, 40).
28. Richard O'Connor, *Black Jack Pershing* (New York, 1961), 113-114. Since less than five hundred men apparently figured in Villa's final raiding party, the number between 1,000 and 1,500 reported south of Columbus must be an overestimate, unless of course some of the Villista contingent remained behind in Mexico. At times Villa also sustained losses from men who defected to Carranza, as, for two earlier examples, the Herrera brothers, Maclovio and Luis.
29. The present account is based partly on documents in the *Pershing Papers,* Box 372, but also on the testimony of Mexican informants who participated in the raid or who had relatives who did so. One idea is that some of the Villistas crossed the line the night of March 8 and regrouped in the morning for the attack.
30. *Ibid.* The Villista *jefe* helping to lead the Raid was, not Hernández, but Nicolás Fernández, some of whose descendants live in Juárez today.
31. W. A. Ganoe, *The History of the United States Army* (New York, 1942), 453. Bill McGaw, "Lt. Lucas' 'Hunch' Cost Lives of Many Villistas at Columbus," *The Southwesterner* (February, 1962), I, 7; but see C. W. Hoffmann, *The Westerners Brand Book* (Los Angeles, Cal., 1959), 17; and especially "Former Mem-

ber of Villa's Bodyguard Settles Old Argument; 364 Bandits Raided Columbus," *El Paso Herald-Post*, February 21, 1962. The figure 485 raiders in the *Pershing Papers* (Box 372) appears reasonably correct; César Reyes Aguirre says 500 (*La Verdad Histórica sobre la Batalla del Carrizal* [San Antonio, Texas, 1916], 2).

32. Alberto Salinas Carranza, *La Expedición Punitiva* (México, D. F., 1936), 101. The allegation sometimes made that a number of Carrancista soldiers joined with the Villistas at the Border Gate to participate in the raid and share in its spoils appears far-fetched, particularly in view of the hour and the detour made by Villa. Actually, it may have been Carranza troops that drove Villa to cross the border for the needs of subsistence. The Mexican President some time before had dispatched General Luis Gutiérrez to quell the Villistas (*For. Rel.*, 1916, 485).

33. *Pershing Papers*, Box 372.

34. Some pioneers (notably Messrs. Vincent Andreas and Jenaro Ceniceros, both of El Paso) maintain that Villa never came to Columbus and that Candelario Cervantes alone should be held responsible for the Raid. At the hour of the onslaught, Villa was allegedly in Casas Grandes or, as some say, in Santa Rosalía. At the opposite extreme, Mrs. Suzie Parks, the telephone operator who informed Deming of the raid, remembered recently that she saw Villa himself outside the switchboard window and "recognized his military cap with the double eagle embroidered above its peak" (Bill McGaw, "Out of the West," *El Paso Herald-Post*, July 29, 1961).

35. Informants: Señor Don José Covarrubias, Juárez; Mrs. Medders, Mountainair, New Mexico. See further, "Wee Wright Boy Brought Safe and Sound to Pearson," *El Paso Morning Times*, March 11, 1916.

36. In the Aultman Collection, Public Library, El Paso, Texas.

37. Frank Tompkins, *Chasing Villa* (Harrisburg, Pa., 1934), 51-58.

38. *Ibid.*, 50; and Louis Stevens, *Here Comes Pancho Villa* (New York, 1930), 282-284.

39. Harris, *op. cit.*, 84-85.

40. "Seventeen Americans Killed by Murderous Villa Raiders in Savage Attack on Columbus," *El Paso Morning Times*, March 10, 1916. It is sometimes asserted that Villa's papers lost in the action contained vengeful exhortations. A long and careful search has failed to uncover any trace of these so-called lost papers of Villa. Mr. Jack Breen (2017 West Wetmore Road, Tucson, Arizona) was born in Columbus and lived there until recently. Having made a painstaking study of the Raid, Mr. Breen has concluded that no such papers ever existed and that the operation was more or less improvised. His conclusion echoes that of his deceased father and that of the late Colonel Rodríguez (both of whom were also interviewed by the author of this study years ago). The elder Breen lived in Columbus at the time of the Raid; Colonel Rodríguez was a Villista who took part in the attack. The present theory is not intended as either a criticism or a defense of Villa but as an explanation of his motive; namely, booty. One noted Mexican historian describes the raid in terms of unbridled bestiality on the part of Villa (Celia Herrera, *Francisco Villa ante la Historia* [2nd ed., México, D. F., 1964], 177).

41. Tompkins, *op. cit.*, 46.

42. *Ibid.*, 53.

43. H. A. Toulmin, *With Pershing in Mexico* (Harrisburg, Pa., 1935), 33-34.

44. *Pershing Papers*, Box 373.

45. *Ibid.*, Tompkins, *op. cit.*, 49-53.

46. I. J. Bush, *Gringo Doctor* (Caldwell, Idaho, 1939), 241-242.

47. Salinas Carranza, *op. cit.*, 107.

48. Bill McGaw, "Lt. Lucas' 'Hunch' Cost Lives of Many Villistas at Columbus," *The Southwesterner* (February, 1962), I, 6.

49. "Private Wounded in Raid at Columbus Loses Arm," *El Paso Morning Times*, March 12, 1916.

50. Tompkins, *op. cit.*, 52.

51. Carl Hawk, "Villa Takes the Town," *The Southwesterner* (March, 1962), I, 6-7.
52. "Boy of Fourteen Saves Brother's Life During Raid on Columbus, N. M.," El Paso *Morning Times*, March 10, 1916.
53. Tompkins, *op. cit.*, 58.
54. *Ibid.*
55. Bill McGaw, "One Columbus Man Wrote Checks for Villistas; They Spared His Life," El Paso *Herald-Post*, July 22, 1961.
56. *Ibid.*
57. Harris, *op. cit.*, 89.
58. Informant: Mr. Jack W. Breen, Jr., Tucson, Arizona.
59. Toulmin, *op. cit.*, 37-38.
60. *Ibid.;* Tompkins, *op. cit.*, 59.
61. Tompkins, *op. cit.*, 58f.
62. *Ibid.*, 59.
63. *Ibid.*, 131-132.
64. See footnote 40.
65. *Ibid.*
66. Informant: Mrs. Maude Hawk Wright Medders, Mountainair, New Mexico.
67. *Ibid.*
68. *Ibid.* "Dramatic Speech by Villa at Palomas Incited His Band of Bandits to Murder Americans," El Paso *Morning Times*, March 15, 1916.
69. "You may go; you are at liberty."
70. For an account of Mrs. Wright's liberation, see the reference in footnote 40.
71. *Ibid.*
72. The foregoing roll of dead and wounded is substantially correct (although A. L. Ritchie is sometimes given for William T. Ritchie); however, no official list appears to exist. The names included in this study were compiled with the help of Mrs. William Birch (1820 East Nevada Street, El Paso, Texas), Mr. Charles H. Culver (Superintendent, Fort Bliss National Cemetery), and Dr. Myra Ellen Jenkins (State Records Center and Archives, Santa Fé, New Mexico).
73. *Pershing Papers,* Box 372. Mr. Leon B. Graves, Ottawa, Kansas, has done special research on the number of Mexican prisoners taken at Columbus and their subsequent fate.
74. Informant: Mr. Jack Zimmatore, Alice, Texas, then a Private in the United States Army.
75. *Pershing Papers,* Box 372.
76. *Ibid.*
77. See footnote 35.
78. Harris, *op. cit.*, 90. A Mexican author says that Villa entered Columbus *"al frente de sus más fieles soldados"* (Pere Foix, *Pancho Villa* [5th ed., México, D. F., 1960], 219).
79. See footnote 68 and Tompkins, *op. cit.*, 62.
80. Saturnino A. Villanueva Zuloaga, Francisco Alvarez Morales, and Jesús Aizpuru Salas, "Para Muestra con un Botón Basta," *Relatos Auténticos de Pancho Villa* (Juárez, Chihuahua, May, 1961), núm. 1, 11-14.
81. Salinas Carranza, *op. cit.*, 106-107.
82. Tompkins, *op. cit.*, 55.
83. *Ibid.*, 56.
84. *Ibid.*
85. In English, "mounted men."
86. Tompkins, *op. cit.*, 56.
87. *Ibid.*
88. Pablo López, one of Villa's top officers, was wounded in both legs.

89. As for the number of his men killed, "Villa afterward admitted his loss to be nearly two hundred" (*Pershing Papers*, Box 373).
90. Tompkins, *op. cit.*, 56.
91. Anita Brenner, *Idols Behind Altars* (New York, 1929), 204.
92. The late Mr. Brown was then a prosperous member of the Mexican Mormon colony. These Mormons found it possible to conduct business with Villa without inviting aggression.
93. According to a noted Mexican historian, Villa had a special interest in stealing the horses of the Yankee garrison (José Vasconcelos, *Breve Historia de México* [México, D. F., 1956], 456).
94. "German Gold as Aid to Strife in Mexico," New York *Evening Telegram*, January 14, 1916; see also Cullom H. Farrell, *Incidents in the Life of General John J. Pershing* (New York, 1918), 96; Everett T. Tomlinson, *The Story of General Pershing* (New York, 1919), 120; O'Connor, *op. cit.*, 112.
95. See McGaw in footnote 16.
96. One contemporary rumor ran that Americans with interests in northern Mexico "had slipped Villa a good fat sum of American dollars," presumably in hopes of bringing the intervention of the United States to protect their investment and assure the safe construction of the *Oriente* railway. (Informant: Mr. Robert N. Mullin, South Laguna, California.) Similar allegations were made a few days after the Raid by the New York Socialist Congressman Meyer London (*Cong. Record*, 64 Cong., 1 sess., 5020-5021) and the *Christian Science Monitor* (March 11, 1916), III, no. 90.
97. Informant: Colonel Manuel Trujillo, Parral, Chihuahua. Trujillo said that the Villistas received arms from both Germany and Japan. Señora Soledad Seañez de Villa, Pancho's last wife, reported in her native Spanish, during an interview in her Juárez home, that "Villa spoke highly of the Germans. Had he known me earlier, he would have sent me to school in Germany. He had a high opinion of the Germans and their machines, and Germans did visit General Villa frequently." From an American source, one learns that the Mexican leader greatly admired the Prussian Marshal Von Hindenburg (Thorkel F. Mortensen, "Will Drive Gen. Pershing Out, Villa Declares in Interview," [New York *World*, December 11, 1916]).
98. This refers to the celebrated Zimmerman telegram, intercepted by the Americans, which directed the German Minister in Mexico City to assure the *de facto* government there of ample inducement for engaging the United States in war.
99. Señor Tomás Gameros, Governor of Chihuahua, issued a decree proscribing Villa and placing a price on his head of one hundred thousand pesos (Señora Luz Corral vda. de Villa, *Pancho Villa en la Intimidad* [México, D. F., 1948], 169).
100. The fact of the matter is that the contending Mexican parties shared a patriotic resolve to settle their affairs among themselves. No figure of the Revolution sought foreign intervention (Informant: Señorita Josefina Hernández, Parral, Chih.).
101. A contemptuous term for Constitutionalist federal policemen, who wore their hair short.
102. The widely-published incident of the transshipment of Carrancista troops by American railway to Douglas, Arizona, in November, 1915, was not the sole such instance of American favoritism hateful to Villa. A subsequent crucial dispensation dated December 13, 1915, has been overlooked: "The State of New Mexico grants permission to the *de facto* Government of Mexico to transport soldiers, arms, ammunition and horses from Nogales, Arizona, to Ojinaga, Chihuahua, or to such other point between Juárez and Ojinaga . . ." (*Mexican Claims Case Files*, Box 6).
103. As for the guerrilla's pressing needs at that time, Deputy Collector of Customs Zachary Lamar Cobb had helped to bring this about when he had earlier "cut off supplies for Villa passing through El Paso . . ." (Clendenen, *op. cit.*, 215).
104. Dr. Roy E. Stivison, then in Columbus as the school principal, notes that many theories have been advanced to explain the assault and then states: "Above them

Pancho Villa at Columbus [43

all stands clearly the fact that Villa intended no general massacre" (Roy E. Stivison with Della Mavity McDonnell, "When Villa Raided Columbus," *New Mexico Magazine* [December, 1950], XXVIII, 43).

105. Lt. Lucas reported to Headquarters that his four machine guns were in action an "hour and a half" (Tompkins, *op. cit.*, 52).

106. William A. Keleher nonetheless voices the popular view that "the attack turned out to be a massacre" in *The Fabulous Frontier* (Santa Fé, N. M., 1945), 115, note. Yet a total of eighteen American dead hardly suggests a massacre, "a general slaughter of human beings" (*The American College Dictionary* [New York, 1961]), 749.

107. Clendenen, *op. cit.*, 245.

108. As a *guerrillero impar*, Villa may have chosen Columbus because "years before" at this town "the Orozquistas had stolen the United States army machine guns" (Turner, *op. cit.*, 251). Villa may have settled upon March 9 for the day of the Raid to mark the anniversary of an important event in the Mexican War (1846-1848). At any rate, Villa's purpose in going to Columbus was not mainly to kill Americans. First, what the Villistas chanted there was not *"Maten los gringos!"* (as legend has it), but the battle-cry of their Conventionist party: *"Viva Villa! Viva México! Maten los Traidores!"* (Edgcumb Pinchon, *Viva Villa!* [New York, 1933], 340). Second, the Villistas did not kill only Americans, as the record would seem to indicate, but they also abducted and killed a young Señor Perera from the Mexican consulate in El Paso (Stivison, *op. cit.*, 37). Finally, a special detail of the raiding party was sent directly to the corrals to drive off horses into Mexico (*ibid.*).

R01 0897 9342

2812-21
22-72